MORE CRICKET SONGS

MORE
CRICKET SONGS.

Japanese haiku
translated by Harry Behn

illustrated with pictures by
Japanese masters

HARCOURT BRACE JOVANOVICH, INC., NEW YORK

One star lingering
low in a mist as slowly
sun warms the treetops.

HARRY BEHN

Has a drift of snow
again covered the same small
lonely hill we knew?

BASHO

7

There goes my best hat
as down comes rain on my bald
pate, plop! plop! Oh well . . .

BASHO

When a cuckoo sings
on the hill, tea-pickers stand
stock-still to listen.

BASHO

A dry leaf drifting
down to earth clings to a strange
green-spotted mushroom.

BASHO

Low clouds are shattered
into small distant fragments
of moonlit mountains.

BASHO

This unimportant
small gray mountain is lifted
aloft in a mist.

BASHO

Hidden by darkness,
even old herons feel safe
from a hungry hawk.

BASHO

The waves are so cold
a rocking gull can scarcely
fold itself to sleep.

BASHO

Trapped in a helmet
hung in a shrine, a cricket
chirps his last command.

BASHO

Swallows, spare those bees
humming westward at evening
laden with honey.

BASHO

Scattered on the sand
like jewels, seashells tangled
in kelp and rubbish . . .

BASHO

The best I have to
offer you is the small size
of the mosquitoes.

In my house this spring
morning, there's nothing . . . that is,
there is everything!

SODO

Wandering, dreaming
in fever dreaming that dreams
wander forever.

BASHO

Our old family dog
trots ahead to show the way
to grandfather's grave.

ISSA

Back in my home town
even the flies aren't afraid
to bite a big man.

ISSA

Restless little flea,
I guess your night seems as long
and lonely as mine.

ISSA

Once upon a time
there was, and is, an old witch . . .
a dry tuft of grass.

ISSA

If my complaining
wife were alive, I might be
out watching the moon.

ISSA

A hundred mountains
echoed in the jeweled eyes
of a dragonfly . . .

ISSA

My tired old nag shakes
his loose skin, scaring away
a white butterfly.

ISSA

20

Look at that strutting
crow in the cornfield . . . as if
he were the farmer!

ISSA

Swinging, swaying grass
tossed by a wind. . . . Spring has gone
and the seeds ripen.

ISSA

Here comes our noble
Mr. Horse! Out of the way,
you common sparrows!

ISSA

Warbler, wipe your feet
neatly, if you please, but not
on the plum petals!

ISSA

Waterfall, only
a foot high, makes a large cool
music at evening . . .

ISSA

Who can stay indoors
on such a day with the sun
dazzling on new snow!

KIKAKU

A bantam rooster
spreading his ruff of feathers
thinks he's a lion!

KIKAKU

There goes a beggar,
bare, except for his robes
of earth and sky.

KIKAKU

How can a creature
as mean as a winter fly
continue to live?

KIKAKU

The crickets are saying,
Kosai the poet is dead,
he no longer sings.

KIKAKU

Late summer evening.
Wind falls still. Cicadas drone.
Swallows fly in sun.

SHIKI

Drifting, feathery
flakes of snow cover the white
mounds of sleeping geese.

SHIKI

Eleven horsemen
ride silently, vanishing
into a blizzard . . .

SHIKI

After thunder goes
rumbling away, the clean, clear
sky smells of hawthorn.

SHIKI

A full moon comes up,
and stars, stars uncountable,
drown in a green sky.

SHIKI

At twilight a bell
booms softly as I enjoy
a ripe persimmon.

SHIKI

Perch in my plum tree,
little warbler! It's an old
custom of your clan.

ONITSURA

A drowsy breeze sighs
and the sky's dry shell is filled
with the voice of pines.

ONITSURA

Hovering above
the brook, a cloud is shattered
by a leaping fish.

ONITSURA

"Please don't go!" I called,
but the fireflies flashed away
deep into darkness.

ONITSURA

Tangled over twigs,
a tattered cobweb glinting
in the dusty sun . . .

ONITSURA

After the goddess
sang, in silence she became
a small, shy green bird.

ONITSURA

With a whispering
hiss, an old scarecrow tosses
straws into the wind.

BONCHO

The ragged phantom
of a cloud ambles after
a slim dancing moon.

BONCHO

Cuckoo, if you must,
cry to the moon, not to me.
I've heard your story.

SOSEKI

Parched by the shrill song
of cicadas, I waken
hot from my noon nap.

SOSEKI

It's not so easy
to leave this cool green garden
for a dusty road.

ANON

A breeze stirs at dawn,
shaking a rain of trembling
dewdrops to the grass.

ASAYASU

Above the meadow
a skylark, singing, flies high,
high into silence.

CHIYO

Now a spring rain falls
gently . . . the world grows greener
and more beautiful.

CHIYO

Even a wise man
can't be sure which end is which
of a resting snail.

KYORAI

I called to the wind,
"Who's there?". . . Whoever it was
still knocks at my gate.

KYORAI

41

Beyond stillness, a
far-off bell drowns the valley
in cool waves of air.

KYORAI

There, where the skylark's
singing crosses the cuckoo's
dark song, there am I.

KYORAI

Watching a petal
falling, a baby almost
looks like a Buddha.

KUBUTSU

Climbing a steep hill
I saw below, on a tree's
top twig, a butterfly.

KWASO

Hills have disappeared
into a haze of snowflakes
that fall whispering.

JOSO

When cherry trees bloom,
woodpeckers bustle about
hunting a dead tree.

JOSO

Pilgrims plod slowly
over a mountain. . . . Above
fly the chanting geese.

RANSETSU

Under a small, cold
winter moon, fields and hills gleam
bald and white as eggs.

RANSETSU

As New Year's Day dawns,
twittering sparrows chatter
like happy people.

RANSETSU

Now that night is gone,
a haze of dew dusts the fur
of caterpillars.

BUSON

Deep in a windless
wood, not one leaf dares to move. . . .
Something is afraid.

BUSON

Slanting, windy rain . . .
umbrella, raincoat, and rain
talking together . . .

BUSON

White and wise and old,
Fuji rises above waves
    and tides of new leaves.

BUSON

Moon moves down the sky
westward as tree-shadows flow
eastward and vanish.

BUSON

Tides of a spring sea,
tide after indolent tide,
  drifting on and on . . .

BUSON

Clouds of morning mist
float over the summer hills
  like a painted dream.

BUSON

Flapping into fog
an angry crow cries hoarsely
for spring to begin.

GYODAI

The chiming river
changes its tune as the cold
bright stars grow brighter.

ROKWA

Who goes there, drifting
in the starlight, whispering,
"Shall I light the lamp?"

ETSUJIN

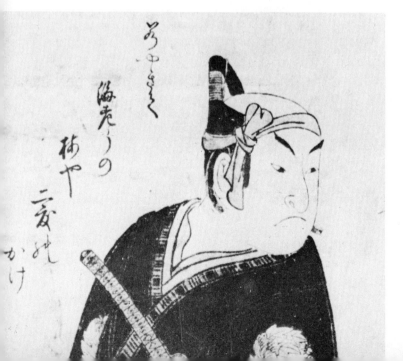

Butterflies, beware!
Needles of pines can be sharp
in a gusty wind.

SHOSEN

O that moon last night!
No wonder everyone needs
an afternoon nap.

TEITOKU

Under a spring mist,
ice and water forgetting
their old difference . . .

TEITOKU

A dry leaf drifting
down to an icy torrent
clings to a green rock.

BOKUSUI

A horsefly mutters
loud in the shining hollow
of a temple bell.

BOKUSUI

When nightingales burst
into song, the sparrows fly
to another tree.

JURIN

Into a forest
I called. . . . The voice in reply
was no voice I knew.

OTSUJI

A wintry blizzard
has captured its first victim . . .
our local scarecrow.

KYOROKU

Resting from the noon
sun, bees hover in the still
shade of a wind-bell.

GONSUI

Hands flat on the ground,
a dignified prince of frogs
rumbles a poem.

SOKAN

Snow, softly, slowly,
settles at dusk in a dance
of white butterflies.

OEHARU

Small bird, forgive me.
I'll hear the end of your song
in some other world.

ANON

The pictures are especially Zen,
most of them now treasures in old
monasteries. They were photographed
by Prescott Behn from books in the
New York and Boston Public Libraries.